The Keys to Success III:
One Step Must Start Each Journey

Terry Sprouse, editor

Planeta Books, LLC
Tucson, Arizona

Copyright ©2019 by Terry Sprouse.

All rights reserved. Printed in the United States of America. Except as permitted under the United States Copyright act of 1976, no part of this book may be reproduced or transmitted in any form or by any means, electronic or mechanical, including photocopying, recording, or by any information storage or retrieval system, without written permission from the copyright holder, except for the inclusion of quotations in a review.

ISBN 978-0-9798566-4-8

This publication is designed to provide accurate and authoritative information in regard to the subject matter covered. It is provided with the understanding that neither the author nor the publisher is engaged in rendering legal, accounting or other professional services. If legal or other expert assistance is required, the services of a competent professional person should be sought.

Published by:
Planeta Books, LLC
Tucson, Arizona

For updates and more resources visit:

www.TerrySprouse.com

Choose being kind over being right and you'll be right every time.

– Richard Carlson

Dedicated to Col. Philip Schultz, USAF (Ret)

As a Toastmaster, one of a kind;
As a man, one of the kindest.

Contents

1. Seize the Moment

Just One 10
    Anon
Genealogy 12
    Stephen P. Mitchell
Truth, A Precious Gem 16
    Arthur G. Lohman
The CIBOTS Among Us 27
    G.L. Smith

2. Cherish Your Dream

Bucket-Less 33
    Becki Kern
Compass 38
    Randy Casarez
I Know You Can Do It 44
    Angelica Sprouse
Turn Frustration Into Creative Energy 49
    Eric Weiss

3. Higher Wisdom

Struck by a Bolt of Inspiration 53
    Cliff Shade
A Day Patrol to Remember 58
    John Grand

My Secret Sauce Bioelectrical Magnetism 63
    James E. Babcock

4. Positive Attitude

What is Healthy For Me? 73
    Janice Boutiette
Persistence is the Key 77
    Albert Anthony Melvin
Crazy Cow! 84
    Terry Sprouse
Outlook 87
    Precilla Leonard

Author Biographies 89

Coming Soon! 101

1
Seize the Moment

My doctors told me I would never walk again.
My mother told me I would. I believed my mother.

Wilma Rudolph

Just One
Anon

One song can spark a moment,
One flower can wake the dream
One tree can start a forest,
One bird can herald spring.

One smile begins a friendship,
One handclasp lifts a soul.
One star can guide a ship at sea,
One word can frame the goal.

One vote can change a nation,
One sunbeam lights a room
One candle wipes out darkness,
One laugh will conquer gloom.

One step must start each journey.
One word must start each prayer.
One hope will raise our spirits,
One touch can show you care.

One voice can speak with wisdom,
One heart can know what's true,
One life can make a difference,
You see, it's up to you!

Genealogy
Stephen P. Mitchell ACS, ALS

To forget one's ancestors is to be a brook without a source, a tree without a root.
– Chinese Proverb

There are two important things about you being you, DNA and genealogy. DNA tells you where your ancestors originated, while genealogy tells more about who they were, what they did, the size of their families and what their life, in general, was like.

Genealogy can be easy to find or it may require some investigative time on your part. In my case, our "Genealogical Family Investigator" (my Mother) only planned on spending a year on ours. Instead, she spent 12 years digging through history and following various leads. She ended with a 350 page document that shows some ancestry in the early 13th century. She also spoke to relatives that we have never seen and that live in countries we have never been to. As you can see, this is NOT necessarily a quick and easy project. However, it can be a very rewarding one.

If, and when, you decide to follow your genealogy, you can be certain you will have to use established resources such as Ancestry.com or the Mormon ancestry library, email, maybe even snail-mail, to follow a lead. These leads may take you back to the 11th or 12th century and if you're lucky, even earlier. You will have some unknowns or "maybes" on your list. Just work with it and don't let that bother you.

While you investigate your family history, you will find some nuggets of information. Some of these nuggets will definitely be funny, some of them heroic, maybe a little disappointing, or just a little downright nasty. A nugget you might find is how many times in your family tree did your parents' linage cross and get married. In my case, over a 715 year history this happened 3 times. The last time was my parents in December, 1943. Depending on which category it fits in, it will still be something that you know about and knowingly keep with you or ignore it because of what it is or how it affects you.

You may find medieval Knights or people in religious positions. Who knows, you may have a Roman Emperor (Nero), Cleopatra, or the Czar of Russia, in your family's ancestral tree. This ancestral tree may even show that Al Capone or John Dillinger might be remotely related to you. It might even show someone in your family had owned slaves or served with the Waffen SS (the military branch of the Nazi Party) during the Second World War.

Of course, you will still find the everyday family who was just doing their part in life. Your genealogy may end up being like mine, just a tree full of people who farmed the land, worked in the factories, maybe even became teamsters driving a team of horses lashed to wagons of various types and hauling whatever needed hauled. Then, when most were asked, they went to war for the country that gave them sanctuary or, in the case of our Civil War, for what they believed in. Did their lives become a big or small part of global history? I don't know about yours, but, mine contributed to both. Only you will be able to answer that question for your family, because you should discover it in your research. Then, and only then, can you really realize just how and why living in those times, to them, was the way it was.

To make your search fun, why not draw a diagram of your family tree? It is always nice to develop this type of diagram to show who is who and whom got married to whom. Then show their children and to whom they married. Don't forget to show dates of birth, death and marriage of every one of them. How about a small narrative about them with all the information in this article included? After all this is supposed to be mostly a continuous line of the family. You may also encounter lost or broken lines of the family tree.

By all means, don't let any of this scare you! After all, it's your family tree that you are building while carry out your investigation! What is there, is there. Regardless of who you find, what years they lived, and what they did. They are all still part of YOU! When you have a chance to absorb all the information that you have assembled, it will enable you to examine where your attitudes and bias's may have originated. It will also assist you in looking at how you think and act.

As Michael Crichton said, "If you don't know history, you don't know anything. You are a leaf that doesn't know it is part of a tree."

Truth, A Precious Gem
Arthur G. Lohman

If you have something to do
But do it not
Then you have nothing to do
But then, that is no excuse

This was one of two thoughts I wrote that were published in 1969 in my High School Anthology. Little did I realize how prophetic these thoughts would be. During my years in school I was not a very successful student. I had trouble comprehending what I read. Homework was more laborious than washing dishes. At least when I washed dishes, I didn't have to rewash them until after they were used again.

Taking tests and quizzes again posed a problem. Either I misread the question and/or I couldn't remember the answer until after the time period had expired. It was only decades later at the *University of Utah* did they find out that I had a *Learning Disability* and later *ADHD*. This helps to explain why when I reached the third grade I could not read. I was fortunate to have graduated high school with a 2.75 grade point average.

I believe that wherever humans live on earth and elsewhere, that there will always be at least one person who will try to coerce others to do their bidding.

Concealed Cryptic

Command
Warp Speed
Deep space
Starship blurs
Man's dark side
Stowaway within

We live in a country that encourages us to do the right thing, whether it directly benefits us or not. By striving to always do so, refutes any argument to have others tell us how to live our lives. In this country, no individual or group of people, nor government official is perfect. They are just as capable of making mistakes (maybe bigger and harder to correct) as you or I are capable of.

Simple Truth

Once lived a simple man
Who read simple books
Wrote simple lines
Spoke simple words

It took a simple man
To see simple truth
Not confused by
Gossiping lies

His headstone reads: Buried
By their lies, truth tells
Their disregard
For liberty

    Living in a society that advocates self-sufficiency, as ours, creates daily needs that individuals or families must satisfy. Failing to have the resources or finances to cope, can overwhelm one's emotional balance. When given a helping hand by others, many are too proud to accept it. Or for other reasons, unwilling to take advantage of help offered.

Weathered Façade

Tears held back
To preserve the rugged exterior

Flooded reservoir of emotions
Spilling over dam built within

Pressure builds
Run-off gates jam shut

Years of stress slowly crack
Then crumbles the wall within

Rampaging floods of emotion
Wash the rugged exterior away

As a teenager I grew up in a time of war and civil upheaval. These turbulent times could precisely describe what was going on in my life as well. My father was an alcoholic and after twelve years of my life on the road, our family of six finally found a place in Utah where we would call home. During this time span, three American leaders were assassinated before my senior year in high school.

President John F. Kennedy, Presidential Candidate Robert F. Kennedy and Reverend Martin Luther King Junior. As a child living at various military bases, from east to west and south to north, anyone who would play with me was my friend. I could not understand how someone could hate someone else so much as to murder him or her, and I still don't. Reverend King, in my mind believed in doing what was right for all. Regardless of whom we were born to, we all deserve to be treated with respect.

He Had A Dream

Martin Luther King Jr. was his name
Not a mere man by that name
But a man with a dream and a heart that bled
When arrows of hate and ignorance felled his fellow man

Wounded he suffered with them
He could not wait for doctors with social healing cures

To come out of their closets
Amidst the flying stinging arrows he searched
For his fellow man who were in need of help

His wounded heart never healed
He never saw his dream come true
He was not the Messiah
But he had the same dream

Martin Luther King Jr. was his name
He was not a mere man with skin of black
He was a man who saw the truth
He did not fear
Man's ignorance

    I grew up very self-conscious. I never thought about where I would be in five years, let alone tomorrow. The day I joined Toastmasters International was my first step in dealing with my self-critical analysis. I learned to evaluate others and be evaluated fairly in a positive constructive environment. Each person has something special to offer this world.

Hidden Wealth

Mining deep within, for gems of wisdom
Polished revealing radiant splendor
When found should I reward a foolish world

Given a chance darkness swallows the sun
If it's warming beauty did not burn so bright

How many luminous facets of knowledge
Will be found burrowing in dark dormant
Unaccessed recesses of heart mind soul

If no one searches shares their treasure
How can a thoughtless world be enlightened
Wisdom sparkles when exposed to sunlight

An ally of darkness I will not be
It needs no help as it tries to engulf
Lights phosphorescent beauty completely

As a former air crewmember, a loadmaster, on the C141 military cargo aircraft, I know the weight that is placed on each crewmember's shoulders. The lives of fellow crewmembers and passengers depend on how professionally you perform your duties, on the ground and in flight. l remember well what happened on September 11th, 2001. That tragic Tuesday morning almost 3,000 innocent men, women, and children were brutally murdered by the actions of 19 assassins.

These assassins were specially trained to hijack passenger jets and pilot them in a coordinated fashion, to be used as weapons of war. Time was an essential part in their plan of deception. The take off times reveal the sophistication of their preparation. The take off times are as follows 7:59 a.m. 8:00 a.m. 8:14 a.m., and 8:20 a.m. all Eastern Standard Time (EST).

All four hijacked passenger jets would be in the air before the first target was struck at 8:47 a.m. EST. There would be no hope of rescue for those aboard these aircraft. The callousness of these men horrendously affected peoples in this country and around the world that day and every day since.

Heroes

On the day of September 11th, 2001, men, women, and children in the air and on the ground were placed horrifically in harm's way. On that fateful day, 19 fanatical murderers hijacked four passenger jets; American Airlines (AA) flight numbers 11, 77, 175 and United Airlines (UA) flight number 93, and targeted them towards the World Trade Center Towers, the Pentagon and an unknown target, very possibly, the White House.

Crewmembers and passengers became hostages aboard fuel-laden missiles, headed to targets to murder thousands more people on the ground. None of them were prepared to deal with such specialized, trained, mass assassins. No innocent person that morning was aware of the hideous intentions of these terrorists. The fact that these four passenger jets were now, mass weapons of destruction, had been deliberately concealed from all.

Deception was an extremely effective tool that the terrorists used, along with box cutters, and a makeshift bomb to coerce unwilling crewmembers and passengers to cooperate with them. Passengers and crew members were compelled to believe that the only way to protect others from a savage and barbaric death was by not confronting the hijackers.

They assumed these fanatics had a political grievance for hijacking their aircraft. Once their demands had been met, then the surviving passengers and crewmembers would be freed and unharmed. Any person, in such a situation, would feel the weight of the safety of others bearing down on their shoulders. They would not act, if it meant the certain death of others. Especially, if out of desperation the terrorists would target the children aboard AA flights 175 and 77. Parents try to protect their children from those who do monstrous things to innocent people. Witnessing such barbaric acts in the confines of an aircraft in flight is a terrifying, nightmarish ordeal. More so for the eight young children who were aboard these passenger jets.

Tuesday the 11th of September 2001 started off with the usual hustle and bustle of traffic and crowded sidewalks in New York City. At 8:47 a.m. Eastern Standard Time (EST) several upper floors of the World Trade Center's North Tower suddenly exploded into a hellish fire, killing and trapping hundreds of people on those floors and the ones above. AA Flight 11 had been deliberately flown into the building.

While the world was still trying to fathom the cause of this tragedy, AA Flight 175, just 16 minutes later, was flown into the upper floors of the World Trade Center's South Tower. Once more, hundreds of additional people were killed and trapped at unreachable heights from the fire engines far below.

The towers at the World Trade Center had been turned into hell, with 6,000 to 10,000, people trapped inside. Fire fighters, law enforcement officers, and volunteers also became entangled in this web of death. They struggled against overwhelming odds, to save as many survivors as possible. They unselfishly did their jobs of saving people from harm and death. As the buildings burned hotter and the flames higher, those who were trapped on the upper floors did not know if they could be rescued in time.

No one knows how many acts of kindness and bravery occurred between those trapped on the upper floors. On that day, no one knew, that miracles had to be performed within minutes and seconds, not days or hours. By 10:28 a.m. both towers had collapsed, one hour and forty-two minutes after the first attack on the North Tower. All those still trapped, and hundreds of rescuers, were killed.

At 9:37 A.M. EST a third passenger jet, AA Flight 77 was flown into the Pentagon outside of Washington, D.C. killing 189 people on the ground and those aboard the aircraft.

Fate can be both cruel and merciful. Had UA Flight 93 not taken off forty-two minutes late and only five minutes before the North Tower was engulfed in flames, the passengers and crew might not have learned, nor had time to plan an attack on these hijackers and thwart, their murderous intentions. At 9:28 a.m. EST the terrorists took control of the aircraft.

Crewmembers and passengers secretly made phone calls to family and the authorities, telling of their plight. Those on the phones were told about the attacks on the World Trade Center Towers. Now the truth was known, as to why this aircraft was hijacked. The passengers and crew knew they had to act. The terrorists were armed, trained and in control of the aircraft.

With little time to act and on their own in the air, the odds were against the passengers. Even if they perished in their revolt, innocent life on the ground might just be saved. Knowing they were losing control of the aircraft, the terrorists crashed the jet at 10:03 a.m. EST into a deserted field near Shanksville, Pennsylvania. There were no survivors among the passengers and crew of the four hijacked aircraft that morning.

The crew and passengers of UA Flight 93 saved many innocent lives by their courage and ingenuity. I firmly believe, that if those on the other three aircraft had known the true intent of these hijackers, they would have emulated the heroic actions of those on Flight 93. This is why those who planned the 9/11 attacks had to deceptively conceal their diabolical intentions from these passengers and crewmembers and from the world.

On that day 2,996 innocent people were killed and over 6,000 injured, including those at the Pentagon. So many acts of bravery occurred in the towers, the Pentagon and on the hijacked aircraft, no living person would ever know the number. All involved that morning, September 11, 2001, believed this to be just another Tuesday morning. Even today, survivors, rescuers and those who lost loved ones still perform acts of bravery and kindness both small and large.

All those so barbarically struck by this horrific event on that day are in my mind, "**Heroes**". They should never be forgotten.

Years after high school, I now realize that success is not measured in size. Just the completion of a small task is a measure of success. You do not need to achieve great things to be a successful person. I close with my second thought published in 1969.

Success is but a state of mind
In which a person lives
Who can say they have achieved it
Unless they know they have

The CIBOTS Among Us

G.L. Smith

The term "CIBOT" (pronounced C-BOUGHT) is a spinoff for a term, like the one used in the 1975 movie "The Stepford Wives". In the movie the men in the town transformed their wives into FEMBOTS who were robotic replicas, programmed to please their husband with their ideal behavior, superior grooming, high fashion appearances and they lacked any ability to think independently, or have any interest in getting involved in events outside the home.

Today we have both sexes that seem to be made into CIBOTS with no souls, hearts, minds or voices to respond to the suffering of others. They turn a blind eye to bad behavior. Their mission is to follow a leader, party or organization that does harm to others and cannot do not respond, because they have been through the conditioning process and are robotic replicas of themselves.

They have been rendered mentally sterile and lack productive independent thoughts. They have become robotic replicas of their former selves. The robotic process has seized their human features and they only work to please and serve their leader, party or organization.

Possible Salvation for Survival

We still see organizations that work to help others, especially children and they operate under the UNICEF (United Nations International Children's Emergency Fund) banner to rescue children or the Bud Billiken clubs to motivate youngsters.

UNICEF

UNICEF was created in 1946 to help children in need. Prior to that time I managed to become bald because of the CIBOT behavior of the Nazi movement in Germany. The end result was a population of little Jewish orphans that were rapidly sent to America. The Jewish orphans in Pennsylvania went to school with us and one day a little girl grabbed my hat and put it on her head. I took it back and placed it on my head and went home. Soon my scalp got sore and scabs formed. I had to get my hair cut off and salve was placed on my head to heal the Tetters (a skin condition characterized by scabs, sores, and tenderness).

What about the little girl that took my hat. Did anyone take care of her Tetters? Was the orphanage able to handle her problems like my family did? They were acting to rescue these children as rapidly as possible and such matters probably seemed minor compared to the massive need to save these orphans.

Today UNICEF sponsors World Children's Day on November 29th, 2019. This is an opportunity for us to work to save and nourish, vulnerable children today.

Bud Billiken Events Around the Country – created by a newspaper man

An organization that appeared in Chicago was the Bud Billiken clubs for children. It worked to encourage them to achieve. A newspaper man, Mr. Robert Abbott launched Bud Billiken Jr., a section for children in the newspaper. The section was named after the Billiken, a Chinese mythical character. The Billiken is the guardian angel of children around the world. Bud Billiken parades were held to celebrate children and to encourage their interest in school, socialization and citizenship.

Mr. Abbott managed to get clubs organized around the county. I attended Achievement Club #33 that was hosted by the wife of a newspaper man in our town. She served us tea in her china cups and we had really meaningful discussions. She opened her house and her heart to us and it helped us to achieve more.

These efforts were made by people with positive action. They were not like the CIBOTS who allowed bad things to happen to others, without lifting a finger to stop such actions. Are today's CIBOTS so filled with fear or admiration of their leaders, who behave badly, that they look the other way when bad things happen. Are they so robotic that they are incapable of doing any kind of positive action for others?

Look into the mirror. Have you become a CIBOT?

As a CIBOT, you might decide to become political and once elected, you can join the ranks of the Lockstep Lizards that follow the Anti-Christ. Here you might find the Lewd King and the Nude Queen.

Our youth can learn their history by checking a photo of the queen, wearing nothing more than a smile in Gentleman's Quarterly 2002 as they look up her name on the internet. Max offers even more astounding photos of her, like the ones that brought down a beauty queen who did a photo shoot with another woman.

As our heads swirl with each new report of events on the news, we look to the hills and think, "How long Lord? How Long Lord can we endure such messy events?"

It's a quagmire that even our Lockstep Lizards want to free themselves from, but cannot.

As we seek salvation, we can only pray that such things never happen again.

We think about a song that was used at political rallies in the 1940's called "Ballad for Americans."

We can update its lyrics to suit us. Here we find an excerpt from the old one:

In 76 The Sky Was Red, and Thunder Rumbled Overhead
And Bad King George Couldn't Sleep in His Bed
And on That Stormy Morn Ole Uncle Sam Was Born.

A possible newer version:

On July 4th the Sound Was Loud, With Fighter Jets up in the Clouds
And the Fetch-Her King Couldn't Sleep in His Bed
And on That Stormy Morn, A Renewed Sam Was Born.

    We could go on and alter the lyrics to include new populations, an expanded array of religions, immigrants and races so that we are ALL the New Americans, who bring about change with our talents and that we ALL obtain a renewed compass to guide us so as to remove ourselves from the influences of the Anti-Christ.

    May the Holy Spirit save us all. Amen

2
Cherish Your Dream

I dream my painting and then I paint my dream.

Vincent van Gogh

Bucket-Less
Becki Kern

No, the title is not a typo! It's more like the declaration of a serial traveler who has never had a Bucket List!

I was sitting at the computer with a jillion thoughts flying in untamed fashion through my mind. I knew myself to be an avid, efficient, and dare I say, joyful list maker. Being a lifelong multi-tasker in my head and heart, my appreciation for lists is legendary (mostly in my own mind, of course.) Why, then, had I never gotten around to making a Bucket List?

For many years I kept separate lists for different events, occasions and areas I wanted to focus on. In what I imagined to be a "natural progression" with stage of life changes, I eventually began to keep one list, with a multitude of sub lists included. That has now become my favorite modus operandi. I've never wanted the list itself, nor the making of it, to supersede my ability to fully enjoy each moment of the myriad of items represented on it.

One of my favorite (of several) hobbies is traveling. At any given time, included somewhere on my list there are usually a couple of trips highlighted. I love last-minute getaways, and can be ready to go at the drop of the proverbial hat. However, I also do quite a bit of long-range planning for upcoming travel. It's important to me that I include the details that are necessary for each pending trip…so I don't get so busy with work and life that I miss some crucial item.

    I'm not a hiker, diver, skier, jumper, climber or spelunker. However, I love long ocean cruises; adore riverboat cruises; enjoy land trips; relish road trips, and can't wait to do a long distance train excursion someday.

    When one knows these two facts about me - my ardent appreciation for lists and my passion for travel - it seems only natural to assume I would have an incredible Bucket List going at all times. Quite the opposite is actually true. I have never had a list, neither electronic, on paper nor in my head, of places I wanted to make sure I got to see.

    I realize it's quite possible that true "list aficionados" would scoff at my lack of having the ultimate documentation of my heart's desires - places I want to visit before I'm called to leave this earth. They may not even let me call myself a real "list maker," or allow me into the exclusive club of such esteemed folks.

    "Why," you ask, "would someone who loves both lists and travel allow herself to remain 'bucket-less'?" It's really very simple. I would have never thought to put on said list the amazing places I have been privileged to visit! Had I named specific locations I could have become so focused on trying to get there that I would have missed, or not appreciated the fantastic sights I have seen.

In *Psalms 37:4*, King David encourages the reader to, "Delight yourself in the Lord, and He will give you the desires of your heart." I can truly say that the Lord knows travel to be one of the desires of my heart. He has granted me the opportunities to experience special destinations and meet incredible people in places I would have *never* thought to put on a Bucket List of any kind.

For instance, I would never have listed New York, Paris, Israel or St. Petersburg, Russia on a list of places to go. In fact, these specifically would have come closer to being on the "I don't really care to go there" list (but I don't even have one of those!) It seems strange that those four spots alone have provided such remarkable memories in my mind.

It was beyond anything even I could dream up to get to see 13 Broadway shows (ON BROADWAY!) in nine days! (No, we didn't take husbands...just a girls' week!) For a musical stage show junkie, it filled my heart to overflowing. A few years later, riding a coach through the blooming canola fields from La Havre to Paris, with a two-hour guided coach tour of the city sights (with it pouring down rain while we were safe and dry inside) was such a treat. Then lunch in a glass-top boat on the Seine, floating by the Tower, with strolling minstrels and Sinatra-style singers...I would have never known to put that on any kind of list. What a very special pleasure that I can go back there in my mind at any time, and relive the experience again.

Over the years I had turned down multiple requests to take folks to the Holy Land, but I never had the desire to go. I wasn't afraid, I just didn't care to make the trip. Then, in 2010, I led a group of 42 people on a 16-day trip. Half of the time was in the Holy Land area, and half in the regions of Germany, Austria and Italy. Never, ever would I have known to add that trip to any kind of list. However, in 2020 I have plans to lead two different groups of travelers on that very same itinerary. Amazing!

When we got to St. Petersburg, via ship, we really didn't have the extra funds for much of an excursion. But, my husband wanted me to get to go to a Russian Tea Room. It was a double blessing for me, because that particular excursion also included a trip to the *matryoshka* doll factory. This life-long doll collector's heart was blessed beyond words. We found out, just before we arrived in St. Petersburg, that we were going to be great grandparents for the first time, so I got a 5-doll stack to commemorate the occasion.

Even I could not have prepared the scripting for these very special non-bucket list trips that were handed to me!

If I had a list, I wouldn't have known to put one other very special spot on it. I would be sad to know I had missed what is perhaps my favorite hamlet of the Bavarian region of southern Germany - Oberammergau. It's definitely one of my favorite European villages. I love it in spring and I love it in fall, with snow or without. I can't get enough of the famous *luftlmalerei* (loof-ta-mal'-or-eye), which are the elaborate paintings on the sides of the buildings; the amazing shops; the local woodcarvings; and the Passion Play Theater.

So, you see...I think everyone should have a Bucket List who wants one. I want them to get to see the places that are near and dear to their hearts. But, apparently some of us do better being Bucket-Less, just going where we get the opportunity to go; seeing the amazing sights along the way; and meeting wonderful people all over the planet.

I've been asked why I seem so focused on world travel, and don't concentrate more on seeing the beauty and wonder of the United States. There are so many wonderful places in our own country that I have enjoyed. However, I imagine the time will come when I am no longer able to cross the oceans. That next stage of life will provide yet another special way to continue to feed my love of travel as I have the time to meander across the States, finding special locations and people along the way. Until then, I'm enjoying a little bit of both worlds.

Whether you are a Bucket-Lister, or a Bucket-Lesser, I truly hope you get to see and do the desires of your heart.

Compass
Randy Casarez

I grew up in the 1980's. Back then, everyone had the own unique style, especially stars like Madonna, George Michael, and Michael Jackson. I loved to watch pro Wrestling. I liked Hulk Hogan, Macho Man Randy Savage, but my favorite wrestler was the Ultimate Warrior.

The reason that I loved the Ultimate Warrior so much was because he was different. He would run into the ring and beat anyone that got in his way. The Ultimate Warrior had this look that nobody had ever seen before. He wore colorful make up.

Although the Ultimate became WWF Heavy Weight championship, he did not have a long career. The most amazing thing is that the Ultimate Warrior became a Motivational Speaker. One of the most memorable things he would say is that everyone has an "internal compass". At the time I did not know what that meant, but now that I'm older I understand what the Ultimate Warrior meant.

We all have a compass inside of us. It is ready to be used. I'm always amazed how people do not realize how smart they are, and the ability they possess to help others grow and succeed.

All of my life I have always struggled with my Learning Disability. I have had to fight for everything. Even though I have graduated from college with four degrees, and I have achieved 3 Distinguished Toastmaster (DTM) Awards, I did not realize how my compass guided me to success.

Since 2012, I had been trying to get assistance from Vocational Rehabilitation to get a better job or maybe to become a Certified Public Accountant (CPA). First, it took five years for anyone to meet with me. Once they met with me they did not want to help me get my CPA. They said because I had my Master's Degree in Accounting.

I tried asking for help to find an accounting job, but the case manager who was assigned to me was mean. The case manager made it a point to make fun of other clients and to tell me about it. I could not believe that Vocational Rehabilitation had hired this guy to help these clients. I will never forget going and telling the Vocational Rehabilitation about this case manager, and they refused to deal with it.

They kept saying, "Randy it is all in your head."

I decided that I was no longer going pursue getting my CPA. Instead I figured I could be more successful as insurance agent. I decided to ask them if they would help me to get an insurance license. At first, everyone at Vocational Rehabilitation thought it was a great idea. One day that all changed. I was asked to meet with a Vocational Rehabilitation supervisor.

I went to the meeting, and I will never forget what she said to me, "Randy we have decided that we are not going to help you. It is clear to us that you do not need help from us. You have Master's Degree in Accounting, and you are a working a full time job."

I could not believe what I was hearing. They kept throwing it in my face that I had a Master's Degree in Accounting. I will never forget how angry I was; I could not stay in the room. Instead I got out of there. It was at that moment that I realized that if you want to be successful in life, there is only one person that can help you. The person is you.

If you get up every day; there is a reason that God has you here on this earth. You are here to help others, and you are here to succeed in life. There is a compass inside each and every one of us. Now is the time to use it.

Throughout my life, I have seen many people that did not use the internal compass. They had all of the talent in world, and in the end they ended being homeless. Instead of using their compass, they turned to drugs and alcohol.

In today's society, many people want the quick fix. Instead of dealing with their problems. They want to wave a magic wand and make their problems go away. Life does not work that way. If you want to be successful then you have to be willing to go through a little pain. What makes a winner is the ability to deal with the pain and keep moving forward. What makes a winner is someone who is always willing to use their compass to guide and lead them in the right decision.

When I think of my years of working in the behavioral health field. I think of this client that was a former pro wrestler. He had a very successful wrestling career, but when he was forced to retire, he became depressed. In fact he began taking drugs and drinking alcohol. He kept trying to get help with many different agencies, but it never worked. Every time things seemed to be getting better, he would fall into deep depression. This client frequently had to be rushed to hospital.

One day, I was scheduled to pick him up for his appointment. As I arrived there, his neighbor was looking at me. I was about to knock on his door, but the neighbor said, "You are not going to find him there; he killed himself last night."

When you are working in the behavioral health field you are not supposed to let things bring you down. However, at that moment it was clear to me that this client did not use his compass. He had all the talent in the world to succeed. It was not any one person that stopped him from succeeding. It was himself. He kept searching for solutions, when he already had all of the answers inside of him.

The Ultimate Warrior died in 2014, but before he died he had chance to meet two of his biggest fans. These two young men were excited to meet the Ultimate Warrior. They interviewed him, and everything was going great. At the end of the interview one of the young men ask the Ultimate

Warrior if he could use him as job reference. The Ultimate Warrior looked surprised, and then he said,

"You can put me down as references, but you have to do something for me."

Of course the young men agreed and the Ultimate Warrior took the two young men on a trip. He didn't tell them where he was taking them. They arrived in the middle of a desert. The Ultimate Warrior tells the two young men to get out of the car. He tells them that they have compass inside of them and it is ready to be used. The Ultimate Warrior just left two young men in the middle of desert. He left without water, food, or cell phone.

At first these two young men did not know what to think, and all of a sudden they realized what the Ultimate Warrior had been telling them. They used their internal compass and they were able to find their way back to the city.

All of us have a compass that is ready to be used, and it is up to us to turn it on. Don't be afraid to use your compass. Internal compass is about believing in yourself. Never doubt yourself, and never let someone tell you that you are stupid. Remember the answer might not come right away, but if you are patient then the answer will come.

When humans want to, they can be the most amazing beings walking on this earth. When you have one of those moments when you feel like everything is falling apart, remember that you have the ability to use your compass.

Use that compass and you will see that you are a true Ultimate Warrior.

I Know You Can Do It!

Angelica Sprouse

"A teacher affects eternity; they can never tell where their influence stops."

Henry Brooks Adams

I have worked as a teacher's assistant for 15 years, mostly in Kindergarten. I love my job because the children are fun, they absorb knowledge like a sponge, they are cute and they are full of energy.

Working with little ones, I learned that one thing you can count on is that they are always honest. They will always tell you what is on their mind. If you don't look good, they will tell you. If you do something wrong, you will hear about it. If they are sad or mad, they will shed tears or put on an angry face.

They way that children feel affects their behavior. When they have negative feelings, I try to help them to deal with it in positive ways.

When they are angry and start hitting or hurting others with their words or actions, I tell them to "use their words instead of their hands."

"You need to talk it out," I say.

"Tell each other what is bothering you or what made you feel mad, or sad," I ask the two children who are involved in a conflict.

I want them to say, "I don't like when you did this to me because that hurts my feelings."

After they talk, they apologize by saying, "I'm sorry. I won't do it again."

Sometimes, to calm them down when they are so frustrated that they cannot speak, "Just breathe in and out," I tell them.

If it's still hard for them to talk it out, I give them time to cool down.

When they do something kind to someone else, I make a big deal about it, to encourage them to keep repeating this behavior. That way they feel really proud of themselves. When they make mistakes, I encourage them by telling them that we all make mistakes, even adults. We just brush off our shoulders and keep moving. Next time we can make better choices.

The students are spontaneous and funny. Once the teacher I work with was teaching a lesson about the Creation of the Earth, in a religion class.

"On the first day, it was very, very dark. And God created . . .," she said.

"A flashlight," a little boy shouted, and everyone laughed.

Ricky was one of my favorite students. He had dark black hair and bright blue eyes. I was drawn to him because Kindergarten was a little hard for him. At first he didn't feel very capable in class. English was his second language so, at first, he was lost and confused. I took it upon myself to help make life easier for Ricky

Once I was testing him to identify the numbers. He was struggling to remember them.

"You can do it. You can do it," I encouraged him,

And he did it. He remembered the numbers. He felt so proud of himself that his face glowed.

I taught Ricky the "jacket trick." Frequently, the kids' jackets would get inside out. It's easy for adults to fix, but difficult for children who have never done it before. I show them how to reach deep inside the jacket and pull one sleeve out, and from there they can straighten the whole jacket out.

Later, when the school year was about to end, Ricky wanted to stay in Kindergarten.

"I don't want to go to first grade. I want to stay here with you," he said.

"You will do a great job in First Grade, just like you are doing in Kindergarten," I told him.

"You have to keep moving ahead. I know you can do it," I said.

A few years later, I was a teacher aid in the fourth grade and Ricky was in the same class. We connected again and our friendship deepened. I wrote him a letter at the end of the year. I said, "I am so glad for the great job you have been doing in 4th grade. I wish you all the best. And always remember, *you can do it.*"

Last year Ricky graduated from 8th grade. He was 13 years old. I had known him for 8 years.

I was back working in the kindergarten classroom one afternoon when I heard someone knocking at the door. It was Ricky.

"Thank you for everything you did. Thank you for always being there to help me," he said, as he gave me a big hug.

"I'm so happy for you. You are graduating and going to high school! You're a big boy now. You have come a long ways since Kindergarten. Come back and visit me again," I said.

Ricky gave me a letter.

Dear Ms. Sprouse,

I will miss you. Thank you for being a part of my life. It is always nice to say hello to you in the hallway. I will never forget the jacket trick you taught me in kindergarten. I will never forget the card you gave me in fourth grade. I will always remember you."

Sincerely, Ricky G.

I haven't seen Ricky since that day. I think about him often. I hope he will come back to Kindergarten and tell me about his success in high school. He will always have a place in my heart.

Turn Frustration into Creative Energy
Eric Weiss

Eventually, all things merge into one, and a river runs through it.

–Norman MacLean

I had carefully planned to leave the house at 8:50 am so that we could arrive at the wedding, of our two friends, well before the 10:00 am start time. However, while my wife and I were ready to go, my two lazy teenage sons were still glued to their beds.

"Get up, you have to shower now in order for us to leave on time," said I to one son.

"It only takes me 10 minutes to take a shower," he mumbled grumpily.

"You're conveniently not counting the time for you to get dressed and eat breakfast," I pointed out.

My other son, responded to me with passive-aggressive silence. He leisurely showered and dressed.

I Grow Irritated

In response to the boys' snail's pace, I expressed my irritation by muttering snide remarks like:

"We're going to be late."

"We should have left 10 minutes ago, just to arrive on time."

Or, my favorite, "I'll wait in the car!"

I might as well as have been speaking Chinese. My comments didn't speed them up one iota and it just made me feel agitated and hostile. My heart was racing.

I thought, what's the point of this? I'm the only one suffering.

I Change My Approach

I would have preferred to arrive early to the wedding, but in truth, the fate of the free world was not hanging in the balance. It didn't matter if we get there 10 minutes early or 10 minutes late. The wedding would still go on and we would still see it.

No amount or cajoling would speed up the boys anyway, so instead of fuming, I sat down at the computer and worked on a story I was in the process of writing. I poured my frustration and nervous energy into the story. I wrote like a man with 10,000 volts of pent up energy passing through me.

By the time the boys were ready to leave, I had completed some great work on my story and, like the cow out to pasture, I felt utterly relaxed.

Fishing – Blessing or Curse?

I experienced a similar incident in my childhood when my dad took my mom, my brother and I camping in the Colorado Rocky Mountains. He really enjoyed fishing and thought everyone else should too.

My dad would say, "My worst day fishing is better than my best day at work."

Yet to me, fishing was as boring as meatloaf, and I was offended that innocent fish were being killed – unless my dad was somehow only catching the guilty ones. Nevertheless, while my dad fished, I turned my attention to nonlethal ways to enjoy nature. I hiked along the river, observed bugs and climbed rocks.

Just Change Gears

It's just a question of responding to exasperating situations by changing gears and directing my energy into creative channels.

3
Higher Wisdom

The work will wait while you show the child the rainbow, but the rainbow won't wait while you do the work.

Patricia Clifford

Struck by a Bolt of Inspiration
Cliff Shade

Do you remember that last time you were tied up in knots because you were facing an overwhelming problem?

Then, out of the blue, at 4:00 in the morning, you wake up and the answer to your problem flashes into your mind.

The really interesting question is, how do you respond to this epiphany? By immediately acting on this inspiration, or ignoring it as fanciful, or not practical, and letting the idea fade from your memory?

Ralph Waldo Emerson said:

"A man should learn to detect and watch that gleam of light which flashes across his mind from within," and "abide by that spontaneous impression" even if the whole world is against you.

While we may under-value this great source of inspiration, there are people who have held onto it with every bit of strength that they have, and that has <u>made all the difference in their lives</u>.

The Artistic Crime of the Century

On August 7, 1974, Phillippe Petit rigged a wire between New York City's World Trade Center Twin Towers and walked back and forth across the 200 foot distance between the world's tallest buildings eight times before he was arrested. He was almost one mile (1,400 feet) above the ground, walking on a 3/4 inch wire.

Policemen sent to apprehend Petit were so awed by the scene unfolding before their eyes that instead of arresting him they watched in amazement. One policeman said, "We thought we'd never see anything like this again in our lifetime."

The "artistic crime of the century" took six years of planning. Petit made several trips to New York for first hand observations. He built a scale model of the towers in France to practice on.

But, as fantastic as the actual feat is, of more interest is how did Petit come by this stupendous obsession?

Petit discovered the World Trade Center in 1968 when he saw an artist's rendition of the yet-to-be-built structure in a magazine while sitting in the waiting room of his dentist's office. Petit was mesmerized by the drawing, and from that moment, tightrope walking between the two twin towers became his life obsession.

He never thought, "How much is this going to cost" or "will this take too much time." He only thought, "I'm going to do it."

I Never Met a Man I Didn't Like

Will Rogers was the single most popular and beloved man of his era. The inscription on his tombstone reads, "I never met a man I didn't like."

Rogers was raised in Claremore, Oklahoma. He worked as a ranch hand and became very good at roping and rope tricks. Because of his magical skills with the rope, he was hired by the owner of a traveling group of entertainers to perform his rope tricks.

While Will was extremely talented, and had many dazzling tricks, he did the show in complete silence. His show was entertaining but he was not one of the top attractions.

What changed Will Rogers from silent rope tricks to international fame as the "Cowboy Philosopher"?

According to his wife, Betty Rogers, the turning point in his career came one night when he was attempting one of his most difficult rope tricks of jumping through the lariat with both feet. This particular night, he only got one foot through the rope, instead of two. The other foot got tangled in the rope. He was embarrassed and made the off-the-cuff remark, "Well, I got all my feet through the rope, except one." The audience exploded in laughter.

Betty said, when that happened a light came on in Will's mind.

From then on, in each performance, Will purposely failed when doing that trick, and each time his funny comment brought the house down.

Will began to include more off-the-cuff humor into his act, and the manager of the show asked Will to introduce the other acts and make humorous comments in the process. His fame grew. He went on to host radio shows, wrote daily newspaper columns, and at the time of his death in 1935, he was the highest paid actor in Hollywood.

Miles to Go Before I Sleep

> ***The woods are lovely, dark and deep,***
> ***But I have promises to keep,***
> ***And miles to go before I sleep,***
> ***And miles to go before I sleep.***

This is the final stanza from Robert Frost's most beloved poem, "Stopping By The Woods on a Snowy Evening."

Frost wrote hundreds of poems but this one is considered his masterpiece.

What inspired Frost to write these haunting words?

Frost said that he had been up all night writing a long poem and had finally finished when he opened the front door and realized it was morning. He went out to view the sunrise and, and in his words, he suddenly got the idea to write the poem "as if I'd had a hallucination" and wrote it in just "a few minutes without strain."

Phillippe Petit, Will Rogers, and Robert Frost, all embraced their bolt of inspiration.

They accepted it without fear or hesitation, allowed it to take over their lives.

Think about this the next time you are in your dentist's office and pick up a magazine to read.

A Day Patrol to Remember
John Grand

I returned to Vietnam for a second tour of duty ten months after I finished my first tour. I was assigned to the same battalion that I served in during my first tour. When I arrived at battalion headquarters, I informed the Battalion Commander that I wanted to be assigned to a combat infantry company. He informed me that he did not have an open command slot and he would assign me as the second battalion Motor Officer.

Basically, I was going to the job of a motor officer while I was waiting for one of the three company commanders, currently in command of a company, to finish his tour of duty rotate home, this would provide a vacant company command slot that I could fill.

Unfortunately, the Armored Personal Carrier that the Charlie Company Commander was using as his command track ran over a land mine and he was killed in action.

I was called to the Battalion Commander's office, informed of what happened to Capt. Crockett and instructed to immediately take command of Charlie Company 2nd Battalion, 47th Infantry, 9th Infantry Division.

As Charlie Company was in the field, I was taken to their current position and introduced myself as their new Company Commander. We started out slow, several short patrols, a shake down to allow me to observe my men in action, get to know the Non-Commissioned Officers and determine strong points and weak points that needed a concerted effort to correct.

As we worked together, getting to know each other, our respect and trust grew into a strong unit that could take on any challenge issued by the Battalion Commander. One day we were directed to a particular area in the Delta region of Vietnam. It was a routine patrol to confirm information gathered by Army Intelligence - of a possibility that a combined North Viennese and Local Viet Cong units may be in our area attempting to infiltrate into Saigon. We were to patrol the designated area and report any signs of a large enemy unit in the area, or a unit that may have passed through this area.

In order to patrol the entire area assigned, we had to cross a river of fast-moving water. From previous water crossings, I knew that many of the men would need assistance to cross the river. I instructed several of the strongest swimmers to position one of our armored personnel carriers (also referred to as a track) at the water's edge and tie a rope to it as our main anchor for a rope line. Two men were assigned to help members of the patrol into the water and ensure they had a strong grip on the rope before they started across. Another two men were assigned to the other side of the river to monitor the men crossing over and provide assistance when needed. Myself and nine others swam across the river to set up security on the far side of the river to ensure the safety of the men crossing over on the rope line.

A member of the team swimming over with me was one of the six Vietnamese personnel assigned to Charlie Company. They were part of the "Chieu Hoi (Open Arms) Program" and known as Kit Carson Scouts or Tiger Scouts. Two were assigned to my command track.

The Chieu Hoi Program was an initiative of the South Vietnamese Government to encourage defection by the Viet Cong and their supporters to the side of the Government during the Vietnam War.

My predecessor had assigned one Tiger Scout to each platoon and two Tiger Scouts to the command track. One acted as a liaison between my company and the senior Tiger Scout assigned to Battalion Headquarters. The second Tiger Scout stayed with me and whenever I looked around, he was only a few feet away from me. His name was Cut, and he turned out to be a very brave man and a good friend.

When we arrived on the far shore, the eight men who accompanied me spread out to pre-designated defense positions, while Cut and I moved toward a trail we spotted while checking out the overall area. I had moved ahead of Cut, while he was checking out a possible bobby trap near a trail that he had spotted. As I moved down the trail, I started going around a short bend in the road. When I looked forward, I saw a man with a rifle, who appeared as shocked to see me as I was to see him. We both raised our rifles to take aim, I managed to get my rifle in position before he did, but my rifle jammed giving the Viet Cong (VC) time to take aim. Thinking I was about to lose this encounter, I felt something hit my right shoulder and simultaneously firing on fully automatic – I saw the VC go down and Cut rush toward him to make sure he was completely out of action.

Cut saved my life that day and to this day I think of him and wonder what happened to him after I finished my tour and returned to the United States. After America agreed to withdraw from Vietnam the news about the people who worked for our troops during the war was not good.

Many were gathered up and either slaughtered or sent to labor camps where they were used as slave laborers to produce food for the Vietnamese population. They were not treated very well and many died from malnutrition and various diseases in a very short time. It pains me to think of the agony my friend Cut may have suffered after America withdrew.

I have mixed emotions about Vietnam, I personally learned a lot about myself during the two tours I spent there. I am proud of the service I provided to the United States of America and I honor and respect the men I served with. On the other hand, I mourn the men and women who made the ultimate sacrifice and those who would never return home.

An unknown Vietnam era soldier left this message for all of us to hear and think about and hopefully understand those of us who served there:

"Here's to us who fought for it, the sheltered shall never know the price, or glory, of freedom."

My Secret Sauce Bio-Electrical Magnetism!
James E. Babcock

Does anyone remember McDonalds and their Secret Sauce? Remember how the sauce was- and probably still is- a vital component in their Big Mac? It was listed in their famous jingle: "Two all-beef patties, special sauce, lettuce, cheese, pickles, and onions on a Sesame seed bun."

Okay, okay...so McDonalds never actually used the term "Secret Sauce". The McDonalds corporation always referred to the stuff as the as "Special Sauce". For some reason, we ordinary working folks nicknamed it their "Secret Sauce".

I'm not sure why, since we all knew it was just Thousand Island dressing. Maybe we were just being sarcastic. But for whatever reason, the term expanded and became a common slang for ANY small ingredient that contributes to one's success.

So here is where "My Secret Sauce" idea comes in. It's something called Bio-Electrical Magnetism (B.E.M.). Seriously B.E.M. really exists. Modern science is hard at studying it. Yet, and here comes the biggest shock of all, "WE" all have it!

B.E.M. originates within our very own cellar structure. You see inside our cells are atoms, which consist of a positive and negative charge. When these interact or mix with the rest of charged cells, a powerful invisible bio-electrical field "aura" is produced, encapsulating our entire bodies.

Now, since I am quite deep into comic lore, I cannot help but wonder if this find would classify me as a possible New X-MAN!? Then before I start to peer over my shoulders to watch out for any Sentinels, as I giggle this silly notion out of my head, the real question comes into play, why does B.E.M. exist and how has it affected my life?

Now comes a point where I am going to be asking you, my readers to take a huge "Leap of Faith" in what I am about to share with you. Since much of the documentation already made on B.E.M. fields are mostly unproven theories. You see what I'm about to reveal has come from how my very own Secret Sauce works is generated from my gut feelings and outcomes of how B.E.M. has had a major importance in my life's matrix.

Imagine this power source is all about our individuality! For example what if our emotional levels of how when we interact with others and ourselves depends on how much of a charge your Sauce puts out, then you'll either becomes an extrovert or an introvert. But when that happens, if like mine, your charge level is that of an Internal Sears Die Hard Battery!

No fooling folks, I know that mine is huge because of what happened in my early 20's as a strange "sleeping anomaly" would literally "shut me down" for days to months at a time. It was as though I was being "turned off" for a reason and once I started learning about B.E.M. I think I now know why, as I learned what a "circuit breaker" is all about.

Much like how "power-strips" work during a lightning storm strike that would cripple if not totally destroy one's computer, if it wasn't saved by the strip turning itself off, before that huge overload struck! Perhaps as far as my B.E.M. field was probably forming, to such a high dose to be released inside me, that my body sensed how vulnerable I was that it just resorted in "shutting me down."

So slowly my body could adjust to its new adjustments it needed to make in me. Then the next bizarre happening came around my mid- thirties when I was returning a battery I had purchased a week ago from a watch repair shop. Because my wrist watch was still not working any better than all the zillion other past watches I've left DEAD in my wake.

However, at this time I was given a bit of "time piece reality." Because this store clerk was able to get me to understand that no amount of anything they could offer me would cure this watch. It Was UNREPARABLE! Because it was a VICTIM of Bio-Electrical Energy! However, before he could go on any further, this shop was filling up with many other patrons that I had to leave and seek my answers someplace else.

So without any thought I drove straight over to my friend, and Cartoon Wing Man, Richard Konkle to find out if in his 23 years in telecommunications for the Air Force had come across anything on this? To which I discovered that Professor Konkle was in the dark about it, too. Thus when all else fails, Internet It! If you have found that you want to be overwhelmed by a topic, just type in Bio-Electrical Magnetism, and prepare to visit Alice in Wonderland!

Thus I wasn't able to quite understand it completely, but since all my B.E.M. did was to kill my wrist watches, I'd be fine with that, since now cell phones can handle the job of keeping me on a sensible time schedule. But, and here comes my gut reaction part, I felt very strongly my B.E.M. actually was just getting started. As my "sleep anomaly" was about to make an unwelcome return, and my wife at this time, Joy, who nursed me through it before, wasn't going to do it again.

Leaving me without any support, I then had to voluntarily put myself in a mental ward until it passed. Except now it didn't even show up, but other things about me were coming to the surface. Nightmares were spawned as dark emotional confusion and distress, with a chaser of anxiety and paranoia, came to light. Then the only way I could ever hope to regain my freedom was to let them give me Lithium, and then they watch me.

What happened next took only minutes to occur, as this weird crackling feeling in my brain was GONE! Of course I didn't know it was even there, until it just stopped! Apparently that drug was able to somehow readjust my inner radio dial that was a tad bit off its station to sync my mind on the correct setting! So was that it? Was this the miracle cure that would fix my problems? Not a chance, it wasn't going to be that easy, as I was released after they diagnosed me as having Manic Depression! However there was another side to Manic Depression: Bi-Polar!

This was without a doubt the best part of this condition. For the fact that I was still a so-so artist, meaning I was good at drawing Lumpy Potato People. Meaning I had not yet gotten to master the human psyche. Thus my forms were rather gross, until my Bi-Polar kicked in, and suddenly I was on FIRE with the desire to DRAW!

This was also a stroke of luck, since I was now classified Seriously Mentally Ill (S.M.I.) and they, my doctors and those at the clinic I was told to work with, encouraged me to use this for Art therapy. But I was still far from being normal as a lot of my mental disorders were the result of my bottom of the barrel self-esteem and heart stopping fear of any type of confrontation with anyone, which left me entering a Co-Dependent life style.

Schizophrenia was the next condition to develop, which I knew from this point if I didn't start to resolve these issues that I was a prime candidate to be a permanent resident in a local mental ward. So I had to start changing many things that was bringing about more mental anguish in my life. The first was to give up my Co-Dependent relationship with my wife, Joy. With this divorce I was literally throwing my security blanket away leaving me quite naked to the outside world!

So joining Al-Anon (Adult Children of Adult Alcoholics) was my first big step in my recovery. What I found there was a family unit, many of us never had before. People willing to talk and be vulnerable with their feelings, which allowed many of us to recognize the similarities, we shared about our lives and beliefs. One's that we were the escape goats our love ones blamed on us for causing them to drink. Which of course this was so ridiculousness that this started many of us to begin our brand new life without shame, remorse or regret!

For me, the smartest thing that helped me recover from my Stinking Thinking, was that I had to, not walk, but JUMP WITH A LEAP OF FAITH TO REACH THE OTHER SIDE! You see I had to trust in a "Power Greater Than Anything I Ever Tried To Do Before", which meant I had to not only Step Out Of My "COMFORT ZONE", But Blow The Bloody Thing To "PIECES"!!!

So my FIRST big step was to join "TOASTMASTERS". Now in my 12th years and counting, I have been able to rack up two completed Competent Communicator Awards, one Advanced Bronze Communicator Award along with one Advanced Bronze Leadership awards. But my greatest accolade was when I was awarded THE OUTSTANDING TOASTMASTER AWARD!

I was literally able to start harnessing this Secret Sauce that was fueling my SMI I was suddenly "Super Sizing My Mind" into creating a number of incredible Original Characters and Comic Stories that were actually going Totally Backwards to what Comics were all about when they first came out.

I sure remember the difference between Right and Wrong as I was a kid, because that's what Comics were all about. However with the birth of Anti- Heroes this simple concept is all but "BLOWN TO HELL"! Which in my opinion has aided to the mess and confusion our youth are in today. Mass Destruction and Zombie Non- Sense is what dancing around in their little heads now. And had I chosen to do these stupid stories I would have made a Truck Load of Money.

But something inside me just said "NO!" And from that decision I decided to breathe New Life into my Own Sliver to Golden Age of Comics! My proof is DYN-A-MIC TALES. Check out my www.patreon.com/jamesbabcock account and see for yourselves how Comics can be Exciting, Fascinating and Fun again!

Finally, So...what started out as a Nightmare as my Bioelectrical Energy was literally Out Of Control, turned out to become the Greatest Gift A Person like myself could have ever asked for. You see I believe we all have been given Gifts, but it's only until you allow yourselves to discover them by walking through your greatest FEARS that you will ever discover them.

God Bless You On Your Own Road To Your Own "SECRET SAUCE"!

4
Positive Actions

Let the beauty of what you love be what you do.

Rumi

What is Healthy For Me?
Janice Boutiette

Let me ask you a question.

Do you think when I was four years old, I told myself "when I grow up I want to be overweight?" This is a story of my weight journey from my perspective.

My weight journey began when I was a small child. My parents were very afraid that my siblings and I were going to be overweight. They struggled with being overweight themselves. They fed us a balanced diet, but no seconds, desserts or snacks. I was always hungry. Fruit became available after we moved to Nicaragua.

It is important to interject here that my relationship with my parents was not healthy and I still can't justify my father's harsh punishment of me. I could not help but distrust my self-image and how eating habits might have gotten off track.

I went to a private high school where food was served family style. There was plenty of food. What happened is that I became aware of how much, or how little, people were eating. Girls ate portions that did not satisfy me, and boys ate a lot. I was always hungry. I take responsibility now for caving to peer pressure and leaving the table hungry.

When I got to college, the food was served cafeteria style. Lots of carbohydrates. I loved it, but gained weight accordingly.

To this day I am still sensitive to how much people around me are eating.

When I was on my own, I gained more weight as I had never learned how to grocery shop and prepare meals. As a young woman, wife and mother, money was scarce, and carbohydrates were inexpensive and filling.

At this point I began my life long struggle. Peer pressure drove me to dieting: *Weight Watchers*, *Diet Workshop*, low carbohydrate diet, vegetarian diets and no white food diets. I could lose the weight but could not maintain the weight loss.

I now realize how typical that dilemma is for many people. One time, I ate one piece of cake and I gained ten pounds! Diets, just like for 99% of us, don't work for me.

I have a long history of family members struggling with their weight. I watched my grandmother, parents and sibling all trying to figure it all out. This is clearly a genetic family situation.

I have spent thousands of dollars on therapy to learn how not to panic when enough food is not available, or more precisely, when it only appears that there is not enough.

What does healthy mean? Who sets up the weight charts? Even now I work very hard to eat healthy. I walk every day and exercise twice weekly. I don't drink soda, eat fast food or buy sweets. I eat three meals a day and two snacks.

I have noticed that food is not the only reason for my weight gain. I was once taking antidepressants and gained 20 pounds in one week! I was put on *metformin* (to lower blood sugar) and gained 50 pounds in a month! Unfortunately, when I stopped the medication the weight did not come off. I still have those pounds.

What I need from my medical community is help with all my health issues. Just blaming me and my effort in my struggle to control my weight is not productive. We need to take a holistic approach that considers diet and my needs.

I have some serious medical issues, but wonder if I would have them if I were skinny? There must be a better way to treat an eating disorder, than the one I experienced, which has been counterproductive. Obesity, I am told, is a personal failing. My weight struggle is even blamed for strains in our health care system. This is very unfair in my case.

I am guided now by the belief that God wants my heart. Body weight and outward image are over-emphasized in our society at the expense of inward character. Believe me when I say that this view of my self-worth and confidence in my self has been one of the biggest battles I ever won for my mental wellbeing.

My God is more interested in how I treat others and my loyalty to His Word rather than my physical weight. Yes, it is my responsibility to strive to stay healthy in the parameters of my body and its needs, not some standardized charts that have failed me.

Now, I have enrolled in a medically assisted program. They are treating all my health issues. I am treated as an individual. All my life has been building up to this wonderful program that I am embracing and moving forward with. I am so thankful for God's help and faithfulness.

Persistence is the Key
Albert Anthony Melvin

The purpose of this essay is to share with the reader my conviction that persistence is one of the keys to a successful life. I will cite five specific stages in my life to prove this point. I have a plaque in my office at home quoting President Calvin Coolidge, who summed up the importance of persistence with these immortal words:

"Persistence…Nothing in the world can take the place of persistence. Talent will not; nothing is more common than unsuccessful men with talent. Genius will not; unrewarded genius is almost a proverb. Education will not; the world is full of educated derelicts. Persistence and determination alone are omnipotent."

I came across this quote later in life, but it confirmed the successes that I had experienced up to that point, and it helped me in setting up future accomplishments. My second favorite quotation in the area of persistence is from British Prime Minister Winston Churchill, who said:

"Never give in. Never give in. Never, never, never, never—in nothing, great or small, large or petty—never give in, except to convictions of honor and good sense. Never yield to force. Never yield to the apparently overwhelming might of the enemy."

These two quotations are favorites of mine because they capture the essence of my successes in life, from my youth to the present time. It is good to remember them when the going gets rough because they help you go the extra mile to capture success. When you go the extra mile, the famous American salesman Zig Ziglar said, you will find the path to be wide open and not heavily traveled.

Youth Organizations

Fortunately, there are many youth organizations available to young boys and girls in grade school and high school to help them learn goal setting, teamwork, and leadership. There are the Boys and Girls Clubs, church youth groups, sports teams, etc. In my case, it was the Boy Scouts of America. The day I turned 11 years old, I signed up to be a Boy Scout. One has to be 11 years old to join.

It took six years of constant, dedicated effort, and in 1961, I became an Eagle Scout. Since 1912, when the award was established, only 2% of eligible Scouts have qualified and been awarded the rank of Eagle. Neil Armstrong, the first man on the moon, was an Eagle Scout.

Of the first 312 American astronauts, 40 were Eagle Scouts. To go through the ranks (Tenderfoot, Second Class, First Class, Star, Life & Eagle) and to earn the required merit badges was my first real exposure to the benefits of persistence. Years later, I learned that being an Eagle Scout probably was a key factor in getting an appointment to the U.S. Merchant Marine Academy at Kings Point, NY.

Challenges at the College Level

My ability to persist over a major challenge came about at Kings Point when I had to repeat the first year, called Plebe Year. There are two courses of instruction at the academy. One is engineering, and the other is deck, with a concentration on navigation and overall vessel operations. After a few months in my first year, it became apparent that I was not cut out to be an engineer. At the end of that year, I was given the choice of leaving the academy or repeating the Plebe Year as a deck cadet. I chose to stay despite having to repeat the heavy indoctrination of the first year.

I have talked to many graduates, over the years, of the five federal academies and most told me that they would never repeat the trials and tribulations of Plebe Year. Most good things in life do not come easy. It took five years for me to graduate, instead of the usual four, but I am pleased that I decided to stay. One reason was I did not have to burden my family with the cost of my college education. An academy education is valued at approximately a half million dollars.

I finished in the upper half of my graduation class. I went on to serve 30 years in the U.S. Naval Reserve (USNR). I urge all young people to consider serving several years in the U.S Armed Forces. I say this because of the discipline they will receive and the education assistance they will earn by going to one of the academies, enrolling in the Reserve Officer Training Corps (ROTC) or earning the G.I. Bill after boot camp. College student debt in the U.S. is now over one trillion dollars and exceeds total credit card debt. This heavy burden can be avoided by earning education assistance through military service.

Promotion in the U.S. Military

When I graduated from the U.S. Merchant Marine Academy, I earned a Bachelor of Science degree, was commissioned as an Ensign in the USNR and received a Third Mate license from the U.S. Coast Guard. Later, I spent eight years at sea and 12 years in the Far East as a businessman working ashore for American shipping companies. During this time, I maintained my affiliation as a USNR officer, even though it was in a non-pay status.

Many of my friends said they would only stay in the USNR if they were in a pay status. When the pay stopped, they left. Even though I was not paid during my two years in Korea and my eight years in Japan, I was assigned to a non-pay volunteer training unit. In this process, I qualified for exchange and commissary privileges, earned retirement points, and got promoted. At least half of my time in the USNR was in non-pay.

I asked a friend of mine, who was a Captain in the USNR, what it would take for me to get promoted to that rank. He said I should serve as a Commanding Officer of three USNR units, earn a diploma from the U.S. Naval War College and obtain a fitness report from an admiral. I did all of those things. Even though I was passed over at least twice, I made it a point to write to the selection board each year, to inform them of my accomplishments for that year.

Finally, in 1994, defying most odds, I was promoted to Captain, the equivalent of full colonel in the Army, Air Force, and USMC. In 1997, I was selected to be the Commander of Maritime Prepositioning Squadron Two on the island of Diego Garcia in the Indian Ocean. I served in that capacity for a year. It was a huge responsibility and was one of the best jobs in my life. Now, in semi-retirement, my wife and I enjoy my USNR retirement pay and Tricare medical benefits. Looking back on my 30 year USNR career, it was worth it, and I would do again, without hesitation. Mentors can be very important to one's success in life.

Unlimited Tonnage Master License

As my brother once said to me, "We learn by doing." The corollary to that is we often learn the hard way. Three years after graduating from Kings Point, I earned my MBA from Thunderbird- The American Graduate School of International Management in Phoenix, Arizona. I never thought that I would go back to sea, and as a result, I let my Third Mate license expire. In 1996, I decided to sit for my Third Mate license again.

After sailing on the California Maritime Academy's training vessel *T/V Golden Bear* as an instructor and Third Mate, I was able to earn my Second Mate license. Upon my return home from Diego Garcia, I earned my Chief Mate's license. Later, after sailing as a Chief Mate on Military Sealift Command survey ships, I was able to earn my unlimited tonnage Master license. It was often hard and difficult, but persistence paid off. I now have my Master license, which I can renew and sail on if our country needs additional merchant marine officers in a national emergency. It's great to have options in life.

Arizona State Senate

In 2002, my wife and I moved from San Mateo, California to SaddleBrooke, Arizona, a golf retirement community on the north side of Tucson, in Pinal County. I eventually became active in local politics as a Precinct Committeeman. In 2004, I decided to run for the elective office of State Senator and embarked on a two-year campaign to win. I won the primary against an incumbent but lost the general election by several hundred votes. As soon as the final vote count was announced, I immediately filed the necessary paperwork to run again. I won the next three elections and served six years as an Arizona State Senator. Always be an educated voter.

Persistence

Based on this personal essay, I am living proof that persistence pays in the long run. I highly recommend it to others. I urge readers of this essay to read the above-noted quotations from time to time and apply them to their own lives wherever and whenever possible.

Crazy Cow!
Terry Sprouse

I never saw a Purple Cow,
I never hope to see one,
But I can tell you, anyhow,
I'd rather see than be one!
-- Gelett Burgess

Most people have a favorable view of cows. We make light of them in poetry, as in the famous "Purple Cow" poem. We even joke about them.

I remember my father telling me, "Terry, you haven't finished your milk. We can't put it back in the cow, you know."

In 1985, I became a Pearce Corps Volunteer in Honduras and that forever changed my point of view of the seemingly humble cow.

My assignment in the Peace Corps was to work with small farmers (5' 5" tall or shorter) in a tiny village in northern Honduras named *La Florida,* meaning "full of flowers". The crops they grew were corn and beans.

My work routine in Honduras consisted of getting up early in the morning, with the chickens, and walk out to farms to collaborate with the farmers. I had to cross the river to reach the fields. There was a large tree trunk laying across the river that served as a bridge.

On either side of the road was tall grass infested with voracious, industrial sized insects that were ready to suck the blood out of my body.

I walked my usual route out of the village. As I approached the river, I hear screaming and shouting up ahead. Then 4 or 5 people from the village were running back towards me shouting "vaca loca, vaca loca. Correle." "Crazy cow. Crazy cow. Run away."

One man told me "Mr. Terry, you cannot cross the river today. There is a cow blocking the road."

I said, "I'll take care of that cow. I will just shoo him away."

"Mr. Terry, for the sake of the entire village do not anger the cow."

"Okay, but have no fear, Terry is here."

I boldly march over to the river. I turn the corner around some trees and my eyes locked on an enormous Schwatzenegger-esque sized cow. As big as a house. He had enormous horns. He scraped the ground with his massive hoof! Steam came out of his nostrils as breathes.

I looked into the eyes of the cow and we had a "mind meld." I could feel his fury and his desire to flip me like a pancake if I tried to cross that stream.

Immediately, my family jewels rose up to my Adam's apple and my misplaced bravado about 'shooing' away the cow, gave way to a feeling of stark raving terror. I stood there trying not to look too horrified. I inched my way back to the villagers.

"Did you shoo the cow away, Mr. Terry?" one villager asked.

"No. for the good of the village, I have revised my plan. Now, I think we need to just give the cow his personal space,"

Just then the cow came around the corner moving towards us. "Arrgggh!" we screamed in unison.

The villagers bolted back to the village so fast that they left a vapor trail.

I jumped over a fence on the side of the road, still thinking I had to see the farmers, and I walked through the insect infected plants. The voracious bugs feasted on my body like a ravished high school football team at an all-you-can-eat Pizza Hut buffet.

I knew these were tough mosquitoes. When I slapped them, they slapped me back.

I managed to circle around behind the cow and limped out to see the farmers.

Later, I dragged myself back to the village. The last few feet I crawled back into my house.

Long after I returned home to the United States, I still harbored a fear of cows. Sometimes I wake up in a cold sweat. How long will I have these horrible memories?

You guessed it, *until the cows come home.*

Outlook
Priscilla Leonard

Forget each kindness that you do
As soon as you have done it.
Forget the praise that falls to you
The moment you have won it.
Forget the slander that you hear
Before you can repeat it.
Forget each slight, each spite, each sheer
Wherever you may meet it.

Remember every kindness done
To you, whate'er its measure.
Remember praise by others won
And pass it on with pleasure.
Remember every promise made
And keep it to the letter.
Remember those who lend you aid
And be a grateful debtor.

Remember all the <u>happiness</u>
That comes your way in living.
Forget each worry and distress;
Be hopeful and forgiving.
Remember good, remember truth,
Remember Heaven's above you,

And you will find, through age and youth,
True joys and hearts to love you.

Author Biographies

James Babcock

The name is Babcock. James E. Babcock. And I have a license to THRILL! Which is what I hope to continue doing as someone who has grown tired of what passes for Comics today. Just because it sells doesn't make it right. So I continue with my "three" man art group to crank out as many "Madame X Incorporated," "Dyn-A-Mic Tales" and "Hero Verses Foes Comics" as I possibly can.

I am a God Fearing man of "58" who's been living in Tucson, Arizona since the age of eight. My art and stories are a big part of how I see what's occurring in our world today and where I fit in. I am handicapped, but I chose not to live the diagnosis of my illness. So I draw, write, and basically have fun chasing after my STAR! Care to take a look?

Webpage: babcockgraphicspress.com.
Email: toons4u@msn.com

Janice E. Boutiette

Janice E. Boutiette was born in San Louis Potosi, Mexico. Her dad was a mining engineer. When she was ten she moved to Bonanza, Nicaragua. At thirteen she was sent to the United States to attend a private high school in Mt. Pleasant, Utah. Then attended college in Glenwood Springs,

Colorado. Then moving to Massachusetts where she lived for forty years. She now lives in Tucson, Arizona.

Email: jebartist072@gmail.com

Randy Casarez

Randy Casarez grew up in Tucson, Arizona. He still resides in Tucson because he loves the heat, and his family live here. Randy started college in August 1999. He graduated from Pima Community College with Associate Degree in Business and Liberal Arts. Randy also graduated from Charter Oak State College with Bachelor's Degree in Business. In 2011, Randy received a Master Degree in Accounting.

Randy also belongs to Toastmasters, where he has received three Distinguished Toastmasters (DTM) awards. The DTM award represents the highest award that Toastmasters can bestow on a member. This award recognizes a superior level of achievement in both communication and leadership. He has self-published one book, entitled "The Big Ones." It is available at Amazon.com. Randy is presently writing a second book, a fictional story about the 2008 presidential election called "Change Is Within You." When Randy is not writing he enjoys going to Toastmasters meetings. It gives him a chance to work on his public speaking skills, and improve on his leadership skills.

Email: randy_casarez@yahoo.com

John Grand

Originally from Hudson, New York, John left home in 1955 to join the United States Army as an enlisted man. During his 9th year in the Army he was accepted in the Army Officer Candidate Program, graduating as a 2nd Lieutenant. John served two tours in Vietnam in the Mechanized Infantry Unit over the period of 1967-1968 and 1969. He retired from the United States Army in 1976 with 21 years of service. After retirement, John worked for a contractor to train the Saudi Arabian National Guard in Modern Mechanized Infantry Tactics. In 1994, while still in Saudi Arabia, he became a member of Toastmasters International. John currently belongs to two Toastmasters clubs in Tucson, Arizona, his home club, Aztec, and a special club he started for U. S. Military Veterans. John currently lives in Green Valley, Arizona with Sylvia, his wife of 37 years.

Email: jgrand5@cox.net

Becki Kern

Becki has been writing, in her mind, since she can remember; and, writing, in the literal sense, from the age of 14. She loves crafting stories, poems, speeches and messages of faith. She is still employed full time, so doesn't have the time to devote to writing as much as she would like. Finally joining a local Toastmasters Club (after 40 years of wishing she could) has given Becki the "excuse" she needed to put more time into her love of writing.

bkern@pantano.church

Pricilla Leonard

Pen name of Emily Perkins Bissell. An American social worker and activist, best remembered for introducing "Christmas Seals" to the United States.

Born on May 31st, 1861 and died on March 8, 1948.

Arthur G. Lohman

Even when you're unaware of having a learning disability, you find ways to learn. In the United States Air Force, Art went from towing aircraft to flying on them as a crewmember. As the loadmaster, he was responsible for the safe on/off loading of the aircraft and the in-flight safety of both cargo and passengers. After leaving the military, he learned a new trade. He completed an electronics course to become an electronics mechanic at Hill Air Force Base, Utah, repairing aircraft instruments and equipment.

He joined Toastmasters International to enhance his communication skills with his superiors and co-workers. In 2005 he successfully completed a 15 month Leadership Development Program. He took classes in management on base as well as at Weber State University. Because of health reasons Art retired in 2006. Although he doesn't consider himself to be a professional writer, he has had several poems published, won several speech contests. He wrote a play that was performed in 2014 at the Fall Toastmaster District 3 Conference. As a young football player, he knew that obstacles could only be overcome, by tackling them.

E-mail: a.lohman@cox.net

Albert Anthony Melvin

Al Melvin is a teacher, writer, and speaker. He never turns down the opportunity to be a public speaker. He teaches logistics courses at Pima Community College. He was an Arizona State Senator (2009-2015). He is a Captain, USNR (Ret.) (1969-1999). He is writing a book titled BECOME A SUCCESS! (For God, Family, Country & Self) to be published in 2020.

Webpages: www.ameri-qic.com
www.almelvin.com
Email: almelvin3@gmail.com

Stephen P. Mitchell

Stephen was born in Columbus, Ohio in December 1947. He graduated from Columbus Central High School (Vocational Division) in 1965. He worked at Timken Roller Bearing Company and US Steel as a Stationary Engineer.

In 1983, Stephen started at Sun Tran, as a Coach Operator, retiring in August 2011. In September 2012, he joined Toastmasters, eventually belonging to three clubs. He currently holds Advanced Communicator Silver and Advanced Leader Silver status. Stephen expects to receive his Distinguished Toastmaster (DTM) award in February 2020.

Email: stephenmitchell830@gmail.com

Cliff Shade

Retired from U.S. Army. Favorite expressions:

"I do more work in the morning than most people do all day long."

"Wouldn't that frost your pipes."

G.L. Smith

G.L. Smith is a former writing instructor for *USAFI* (United States Armed Forces Institute). She taught Freshman English and Rhetoric. Ms. Smith enjoys working with students on creative writing projects.

She collaborated with an interesting class of foreign high school students who revised *Dante's Inferno* and inserted the leaders and villains of their countries in various levels in the underworld, for punishment of their misdeeds.

Email: trailstone@aol.com

Angelica Sprouse

Angelica is a teacher aid in Kindergarten. She has two grown boys of her own who keep her busy because they still act like teenagers. Angelica likes to plant flowers, go to exercise classes, read books and play with Bella the cat.

The student editors of the 2017 St. Cyril School Yearbook dedicated it to Angelica. It reads, "Mrs. Sprouse is known for her caring and patient work. She is gentle, helpful and nurturing. She can be seen out at lunch tables helping little ones open their lunch items, comforting a kinder student, wiping away a tear, and bandaging a scraped knee."

Terry Sprouse

Terry Sprouse is a speaker, storyteller, and Lincoln-ologist. Ever since reading Carl Sandburg's "Abraham Lincoln," which fortuitously fell into his hands as a literature-starved Peace Corps Volunteer in Honduras in 1986, he has been captivated and inspired by this legendary figure. Terry now delivers speeches and seminars to groups about Mr. Lincoln's storytelling, periodically turning up on radio or television interview shows. Terry has published five books and is a winner of the *USA Best Book Award*. He adheres to Lincoln's belief that "A story the shortest path between a stranger and a friend."

Webpage: www.TerrySprouse.com
YouTube channel: https://goo.gl/ciXqh6
National Speakers Association page:
https://goo.gl/sTGV44
Email: tsx15@hotmail.com

Eric Weiss

Erik Weiss grew up working in a circus where he learned to entertain others with magic tricks. He now spends his time reading, writing and traveling with his wife Bess.

Adopt the pace of nature: her secret is patience.

-- Ralph Waldo Emerson

Coming Soon!

The Keys to Success, Part IV

www.ingramcontent.com/pod-product-compliance
Lightning Source LLC
Chambersburg PA
CBHW031201090426
42736CB00009B/752